Nana's Adventures in Heaven
Copyright © 2012 by Natachia Dod

All Rights Reserved
No part of this book, written word or artistic drawings, may be duplicated, reproduced, distributed, printed or electronic form, scanned or replicated without written permission.

ISBN-13:
978-1479259755

ISBN-10:
1479259756

This Book is Dedicated to:

Brooke and Michael Kokowicz
The most inspirational grandchildren whose prayers
were answered by God and gave their Nana
a profound belief in Heaven.

Victoria Dodd-Kania
For the countless hours creating and publishing my
dream and believing in me.

Simone Sparks
For believing in my dream and the encouragement to
write and illustrate my book.

Introduction

Heaven is almost indescribable and filled with so much love I had to share and comfort others.

Why I wrote this story… I had been sick with cancer for a long time and was saddened to think of the end. My future looked bleak and I was doubtful about the afterlife and was never very sure of Heaven and what it would be like which is why this hit me so hard. I began to pray and pray very hard for God to grant me the end of my life. I was so tired of suffering, feeling ill and continuing with chemotherapy. I was ready to quit it all when one day my grandchildren came to visit me. My appearance was not what they were expecting to see. I sat there with no hair, dark eyes and extremely thin from the weight I lost. That night when they left I was terribly sad and prayed for God to end my life, but was afraid of what the afterlife was to hold for me. Unbeknownst to me that night my grandchildren prayed very hard for me to get well. As I fell asleep that night I had the most vivid and very real dream about heaven. The happiness I felt filled my heart and soul. I can barely explain the amount of joy, love and most importantly health I felt.

When I awoke the next morning I was sad to discover I wasn't there anymore, but the thought came to me as if God spoke directly to me…write it for your grandchildren. This book describes the sights, brilliant colors and things I saw on my brief visit to heaven. I dedicate this book to my grandchildren and all children so they may know that their loved ones are beyond happy and they are in the most wonderful place they can imagine. It is a place where love flows beyond measure and where we look on our loved ones left behind. It is a wonderful place where one day I will return and pray it gives love and hope to all who read it.

Nana's Adventures

In Heaven

By: Natachia Dodd

"Nana Open your eyes!"

"Wow! I feel so good and happy." Nana exclaimed.

"Where am I?"

"You are in heaven," came the most comforting voice Nana had ever heard.

"Is that you God?" asked Nana.

The light was so bright that Nana couldn't see God.

"Yes my child it's me." Nana could hear God's voice.

"Why can't I see you?" asked Nana.

"You will when you adjust to the light."
And she did!

Her heart swelled with so much love. "When you want to see me at any time, just call," said God and he disappeared.

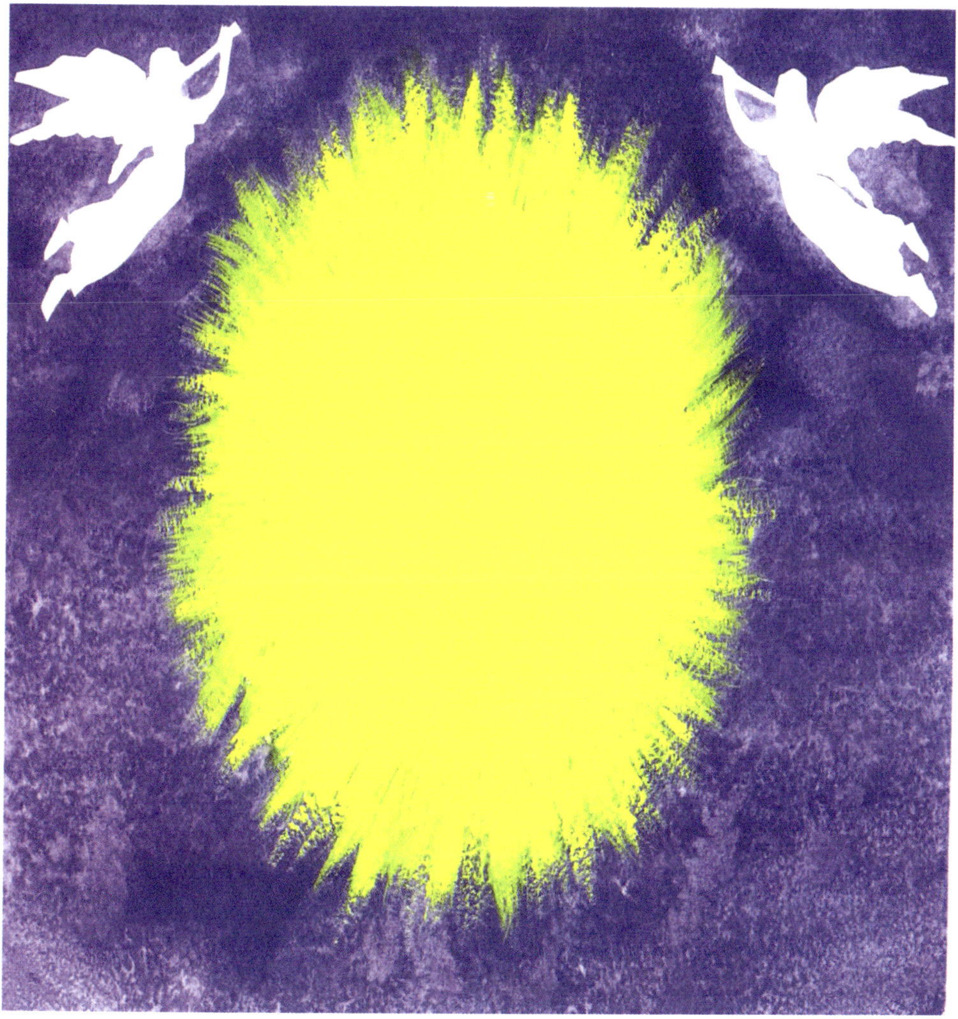

"Oh look! That's my dog, Foxy and my cat, Snowy." Nana was so excited to see them.

"Hey Nana. We have been waiting for you," Foxy said.

Nana said with surprise, "You can talk to me?"

"Yes. Here in Heaven we can all talk to each other," explained Foxy.

Just then a blue bird flew down onto Nana's shoulder and sang a beautiful song and said, "Welcome Nana! We are here to take you to one of your heavens."

"One?" asked Nana.

"You have as many as you need," said Foxy.

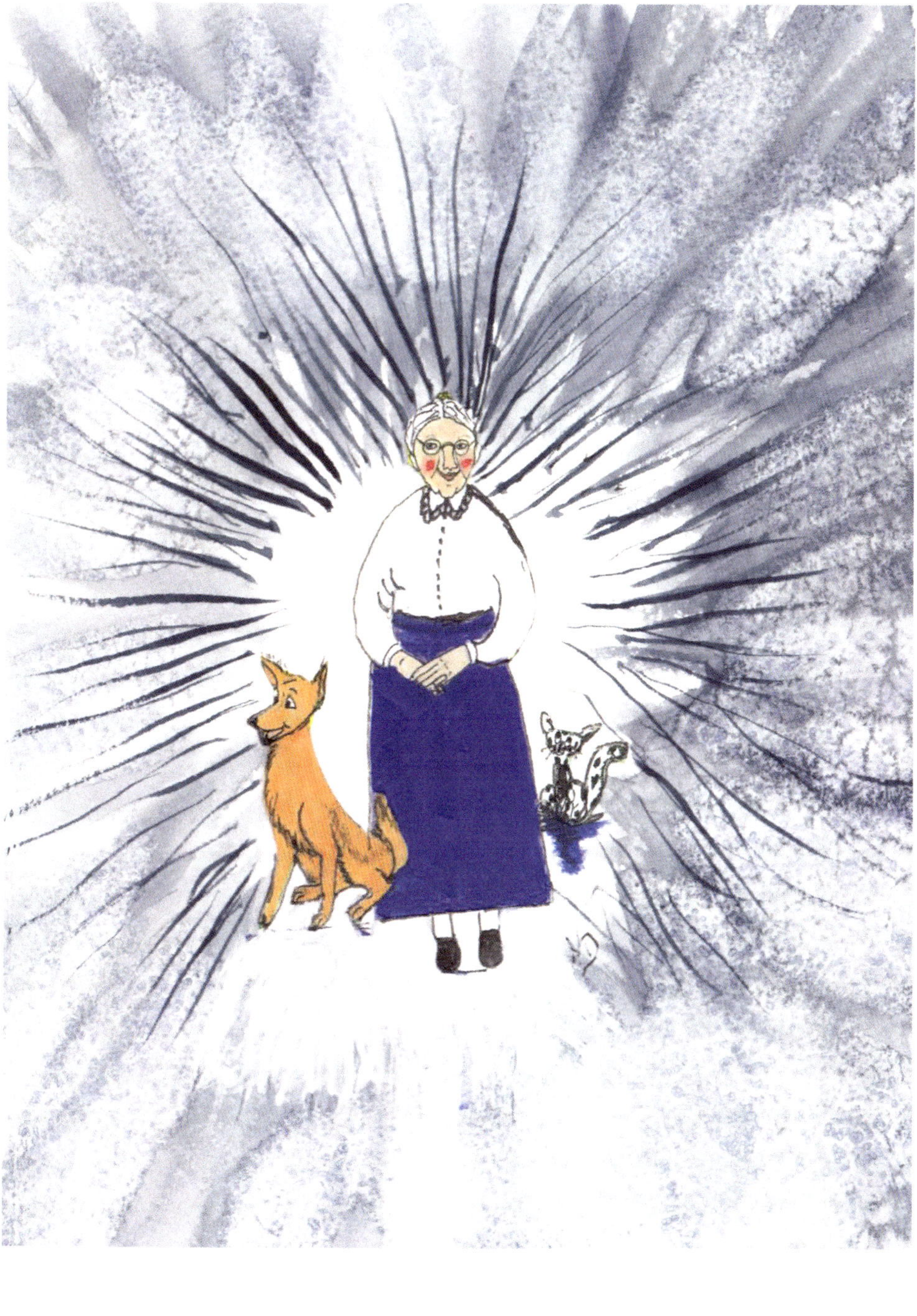

Nana, Foxy and Snowy started walking down a beautiful country road with the smell of honeysuckle everywhere.

They walked by a patch of yellow Black Eyed Susan flowers.

The flowers were swaying back and forth in the breeze and humming a sweet tune.

Nana smiled and smelled the sweet fragrance with so much joy in her heart.

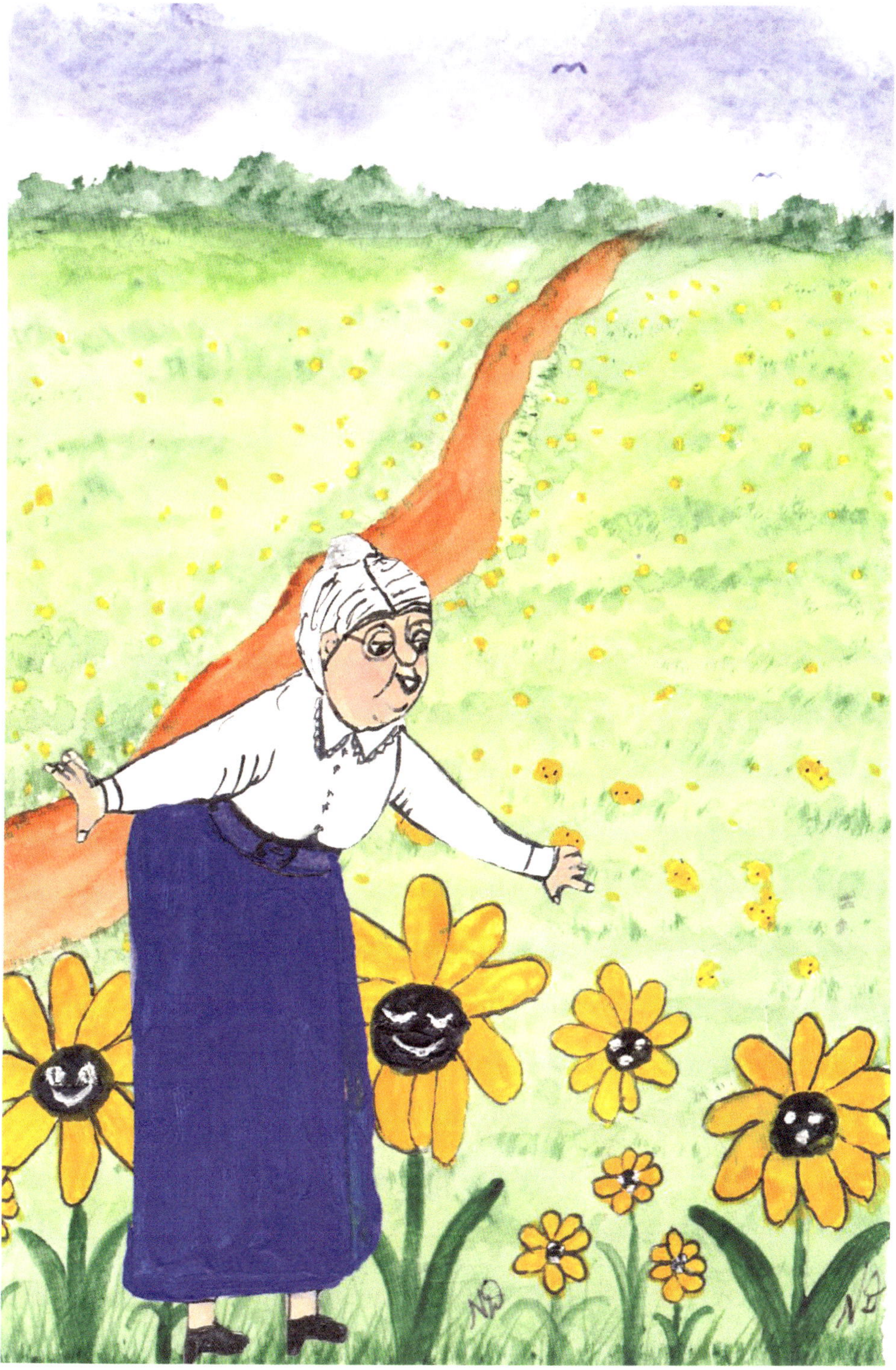

They continued walking and came upon big oak trees and Nana spotted a weeping willow tree nestled in them.

"Hi Nana," called the Weeping Willow. "Welcome to your Heaven."

Nana walked up to the Willow and said, "I thought Weeping Willows were supposed to be sad and weeping?"

"Not here! Look I can sing and dance!" And that's just what he did. He lifted his hanging branches and did an Irish jig. Nana laughed so hard and clapped her hands to the music that seemed to come out of nowhere.

Foxy said, "Nana we must be going now."
Snowy chimed in, "Meow, yes lets go."
Nana exclaimed, "I feel so happy! Oh my goodness. Look at all those beautiful butterflies coming our way. Look at the all their different colors!"

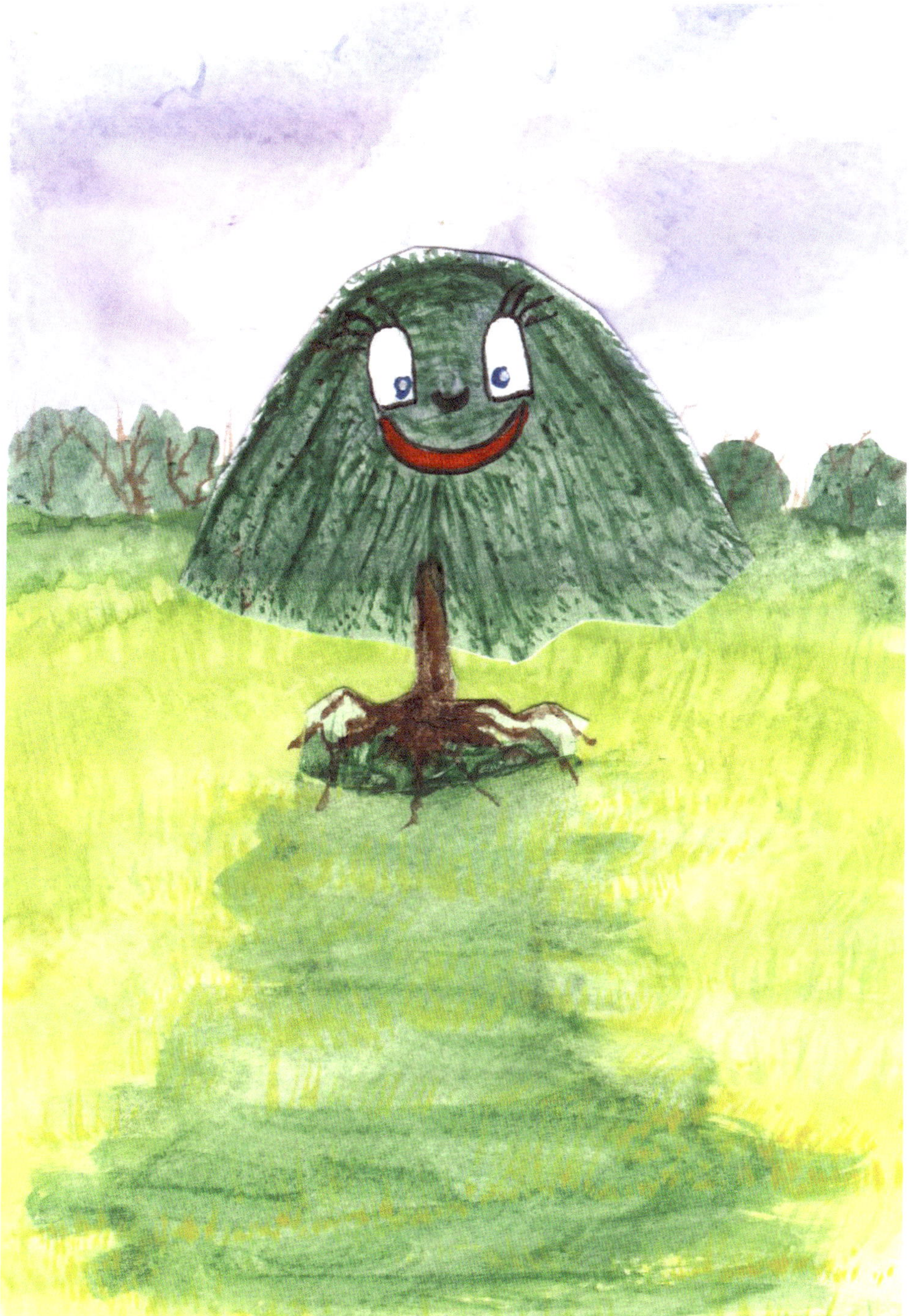

The butterflies fluttered around Nana and began to sing, "Oh what a beautiful day. We are so glad to see you. We hope we make today special for you!"

"Oh you have," said Nana.

As they walked on down the road Nana saw a man in the distance surrounded by all kinds of animals. They sat near a big boat.

"What is that?" asked Nana.

"That's Noah and his Ark. He visits the animals every day," said Snowy. "They sit and talk and he tells them stories about the flood. They love to hear how all survived because he built the Ark."

"Wow! I must come back here sometime to hear him tell the stories," Nana exclaimed.

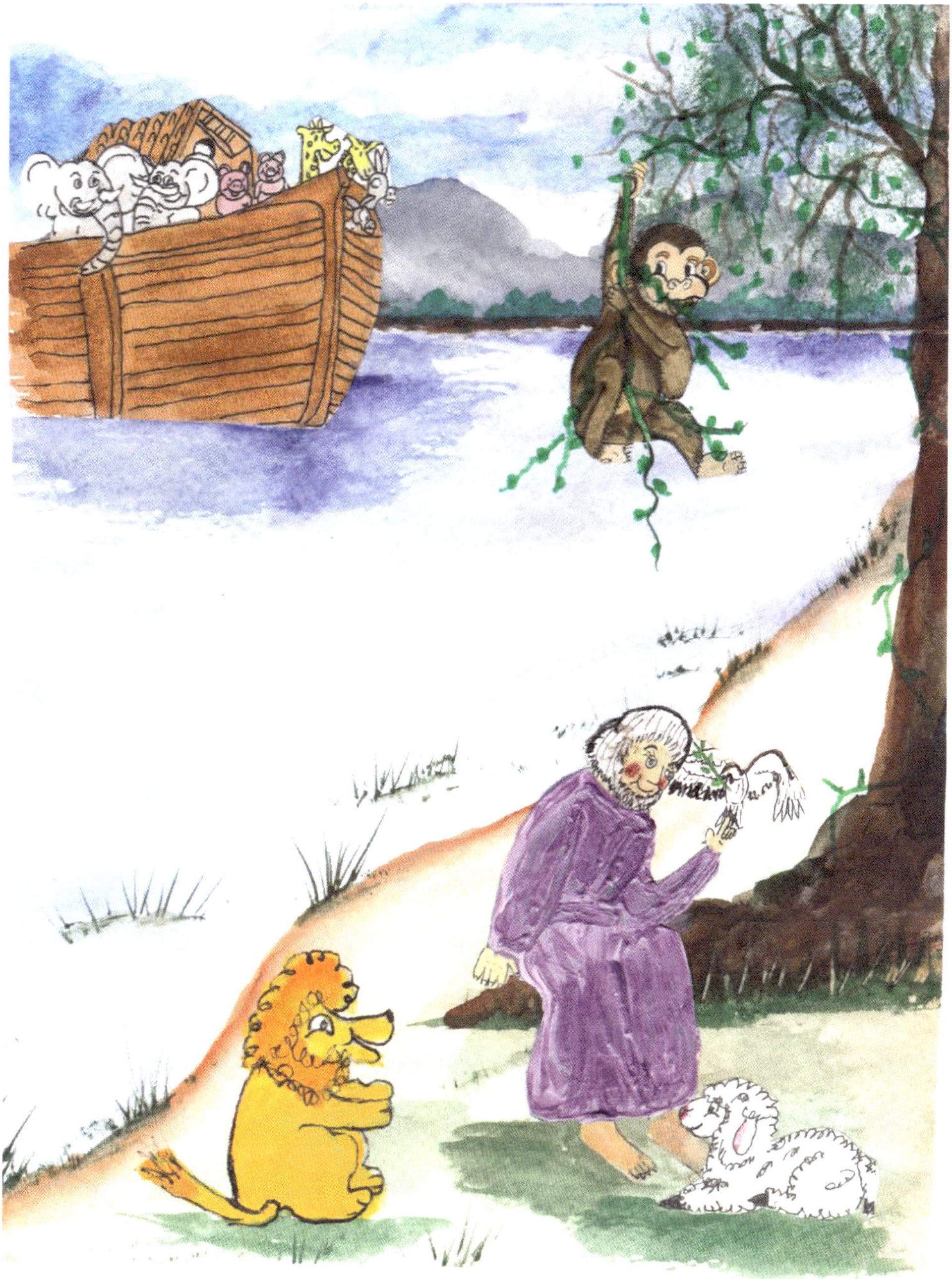

Nana, Foxy and Snowy continued their walk down the winding road until they came to a lane that led to a big old farm house with a porch that wrapped all the way around.

There were people sitting on the porch, rocking in the rocking chairs and sipping lemonade and iced tea. All around the house were beautiful gardens of colorful flowers and vegetable gardens.

Nana looked around and saw many people walking through the gardens and they were talking and laughing while others were singing.

Snowy said, "Meow Nana. Come with me. I want you to meet someone special."

They walked up to an old farmer in overalls and a straw hat.

Foxy said, "Hi Peter. We brought Nana."

"Well Nana. We have been waiting for you," Peter said. "I am so happy you are here. Come with me Nana I want to show you something."

Peter led Nana to a very large garden filled with many colorful vegetables.

Nana always loved to grow flowers and vegetables. She was excited to see such a large and colorful garden.

Both Miss Tomato and Mr. Cucumber laughed and winked at each other.

Miss Tomato said, "Well here are the Bean Sisters and they sing quite nice."

The beans began to sing and sway back and forth. Nana smiled and said, "This is so much fun! I feel so happy and healthy."

Peter said, "That's what Heaven is all about."

Nana looked across the lane and could see a rainbow of colorful flowers. It was all of Nana's favorite flowers. She could see roses, tulips, lavender, lilacs, daffodils, pansies and hundreds of others.

Nana could hear the flowers calling to her, "Come over here. Welcome Nana."

"Thank you so much," Nana said. "You are all so beautiful and you smell so sweet too."

Peter said, "Nana let's walk up to the house and sit in the rockers and I will bring you something to drink."

They all walked over to the old farm house and sat on the porch. Nana settled into a rocking chair with Foxy and Snowy next to her. Peter brought iced tea to Nana, a bowl of milk for Snowy and a bowl of water for Foxy.

Peter sat with them and they all talked for a while and he introduced Nana to all the Pop pops, Nanas, Grandfathers, Grandmothers and all the people sitting on the porch.

Nana thought everyone was so nice and happy.

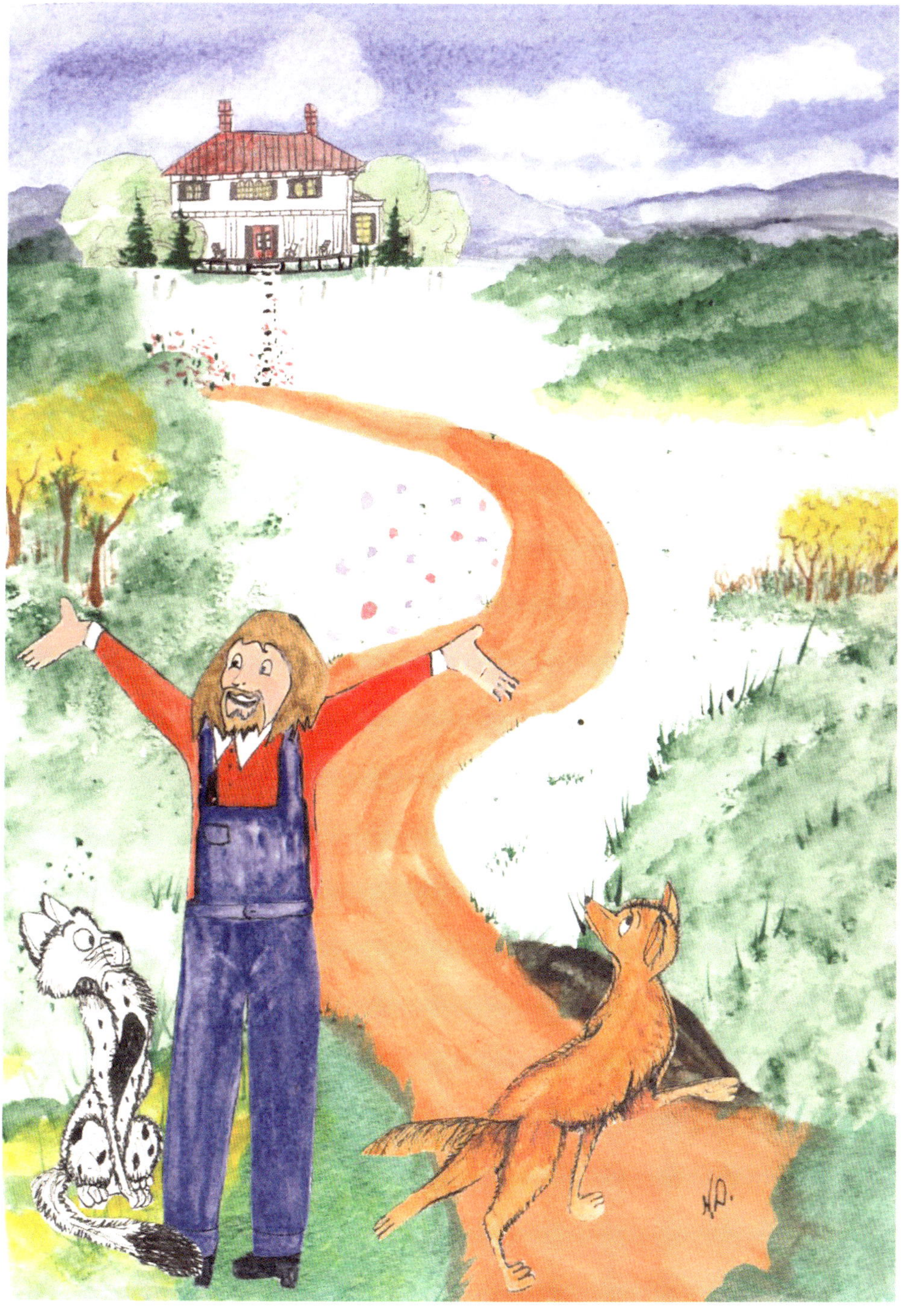

After a while Peter said, "Let's go down to the lake and fish."

Nana was surprised, "We fish here, in Heaven?"

Peter said, "Sort of. Follow me." He grabbed a pole with a long red ribbon on the end of the line. All of them stood up and walked down to the lake together. Peter cast the line into the water and a big old fish grabbed the red ribbon with his fins. Peter pulled him out and sat him on a rock by Nana.

"Hi Nana. I'm Mr. Fins and we are so glad that you are here. On Earth we lived in your pond. You would feed us every day and we loved you for that."

"Oh Mr. Fins. I remember you. You were the biggest fish in the pond and I named you Mr. Fins. It is so great to be able to talk to you," Nana said with a smile.

Mr. Fins whistled and all the fish popped their heads out of the water and said, "Welcome Nana."

Nana said, "Peter this is so wonderful and I feel so happy."

Peter said, "Well it's time for me to put Mr. Fins back in the water and head back to the house and watch the sun set.

Nana cheered, "We have sunsets in Heaven?"

Peter replied, "Isn't that one of your favorite things?"
"Oh yes," Nana said.

Nana looked at Mr. Fins in the pond and waved goodbye as they headed back to the house to sit on the rockers and watch the sunset.

As they sat and rocked Nana saw the most beautiful sunset she had ever seen. It was every color Nana could think of with bright rays of light. Nana was so excited that she could barely sit still. When the sunset finished setting everyone clapped and cheered.

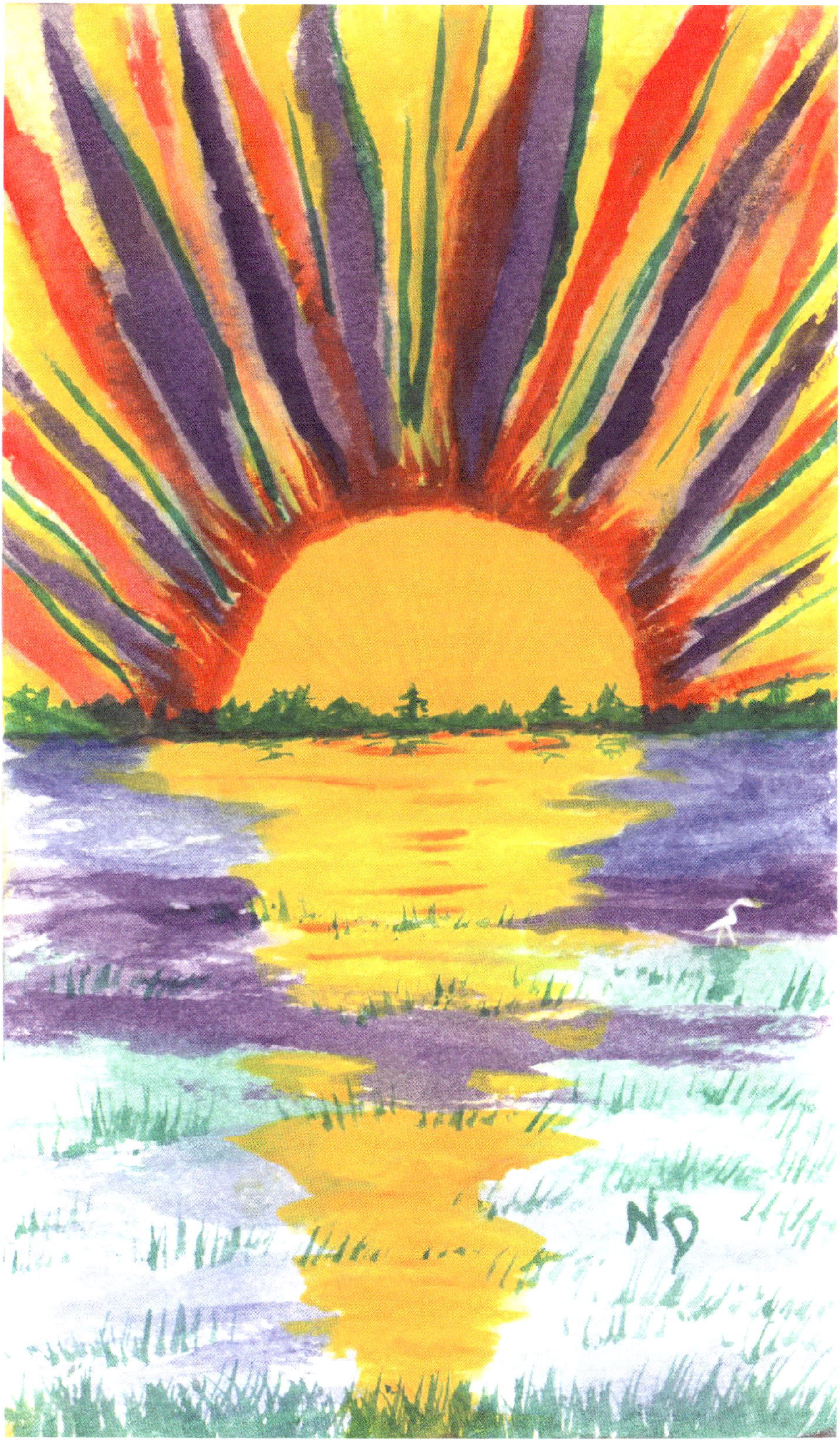
ND

Peter turned to Nana and said, "Now it's time to go to bed. Your name will be on the door. I remember that you loved to paint so there are paints and an easel in your room too. Good night Nana."

Nana, Foxy and Snowy all went to Nana's room. Nana was so happy to find her paints. They all climbed into the fluffiest and comfortable bed Nana had ever slept in. A mocking bird flew into the open window and said, "I am here to sing you to sleep." And that's just what he did.

The next morning came with a knock on the door. "Wake up." Nana could hear it was Peter. "We have a wonderful day ahead of us. Bring your paints and easel with you."

Nana, Foxy and Snowy rolled out of the bed and followed Peter down the lane. The flowers and vegetables in the garden were all saying, "Good morning Nana."

People were everywhere walking in the gardens, smelling flowers, singing, whistling and waving to Nana.

Foxy said, "Everyone here is so happy and friendly."

"Yes," said Peter. "That is what Heaven is like." As they walked down the clay road Nana enjoyed talking, laughing and having a wonderful time. She noticed a group of bumblebees and could hear them humming a sweet tune.

Nana took a deep breath and said to Peter, "I feel like a child again."

He replied, "Yes. Isn't this a great day filled with all your favorite things?"

Nana began to notice that the path they were on was turning to white sand. Just then a big white seagull flew over. "Hi Nana. We have been waiting for you." He flew over her head in a circle and many more seagulls joined him. Peter led Nana over a white sand dune and Nana was so excited, "It's the ocean!"

"Yes. Isn't that one of your favorite things?" said Peter.

"Oh Yes," exclaimed Nana.
Peter explained, "Well, this is your next Heaven."

"How many do I have?" Nana asked.

"As many as you need to make you happy," Peter explained. "Now go down to the beach and set up your paints.

Nana took her paints and began to create as Foxy and Snowy played together in the water.

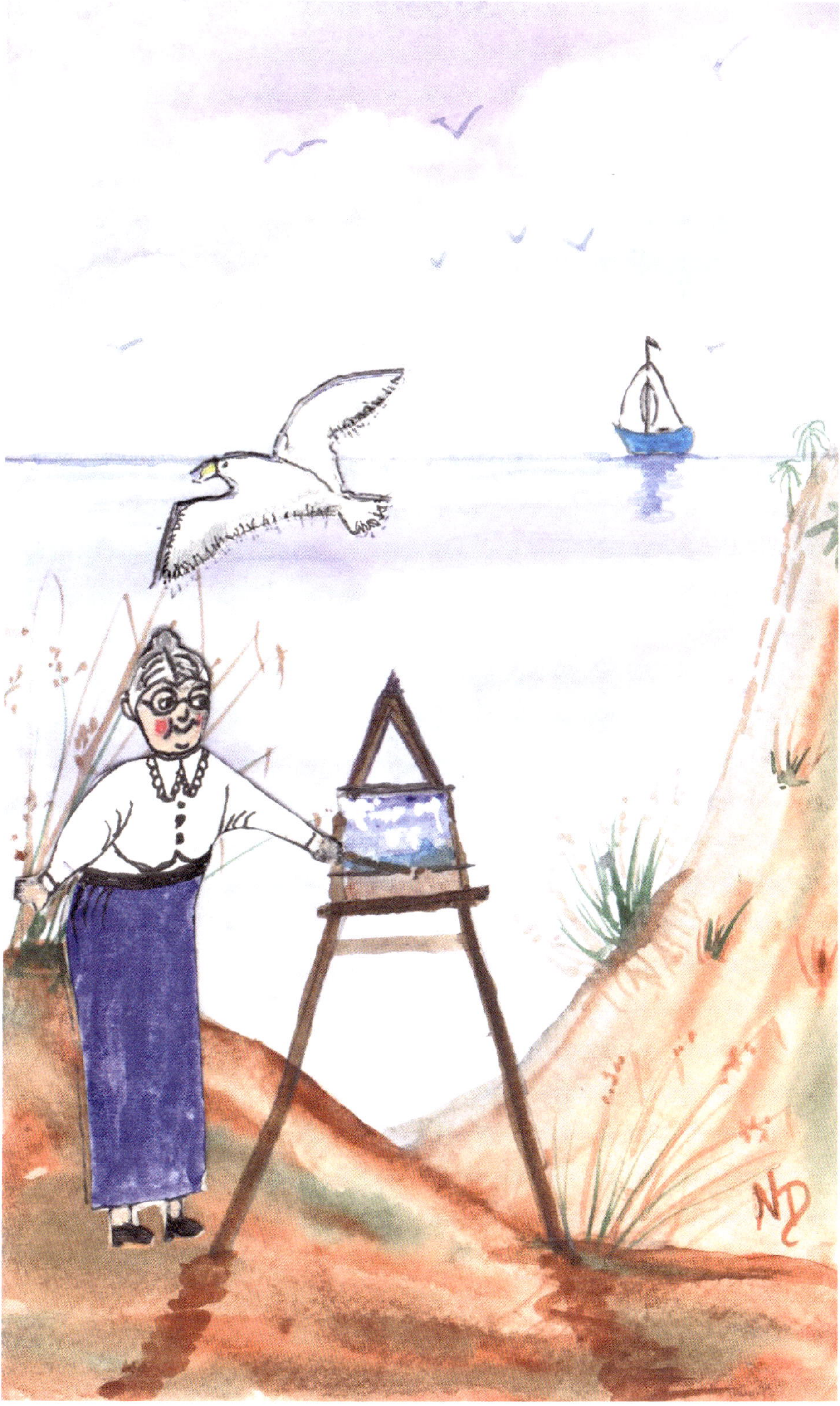

They all spent the day playing and enjoying the warm sunshine.

Peter said, "I have to go back to the farm to greet new arrivals. You can come back there anytime you want." Peter started back up the path to the sand dune and waved goodbye to Nana, Foxy and Snowy.

Nana stopped Peter and said, "Wait! Can I go to the mountains too?

"Of course", said Peter. "Just walked up this path and you will see the way."

So Nana, Foxy and Snowy walked to the mountains and saw they were so beautiful with fall colors just the way Nana loves it. They walked through beautiful trails. It was a great day with blustery skies and white fluffy clouds. They came upon a high waterfall. Time to sit and just enjoy all this beauty", Nana said.

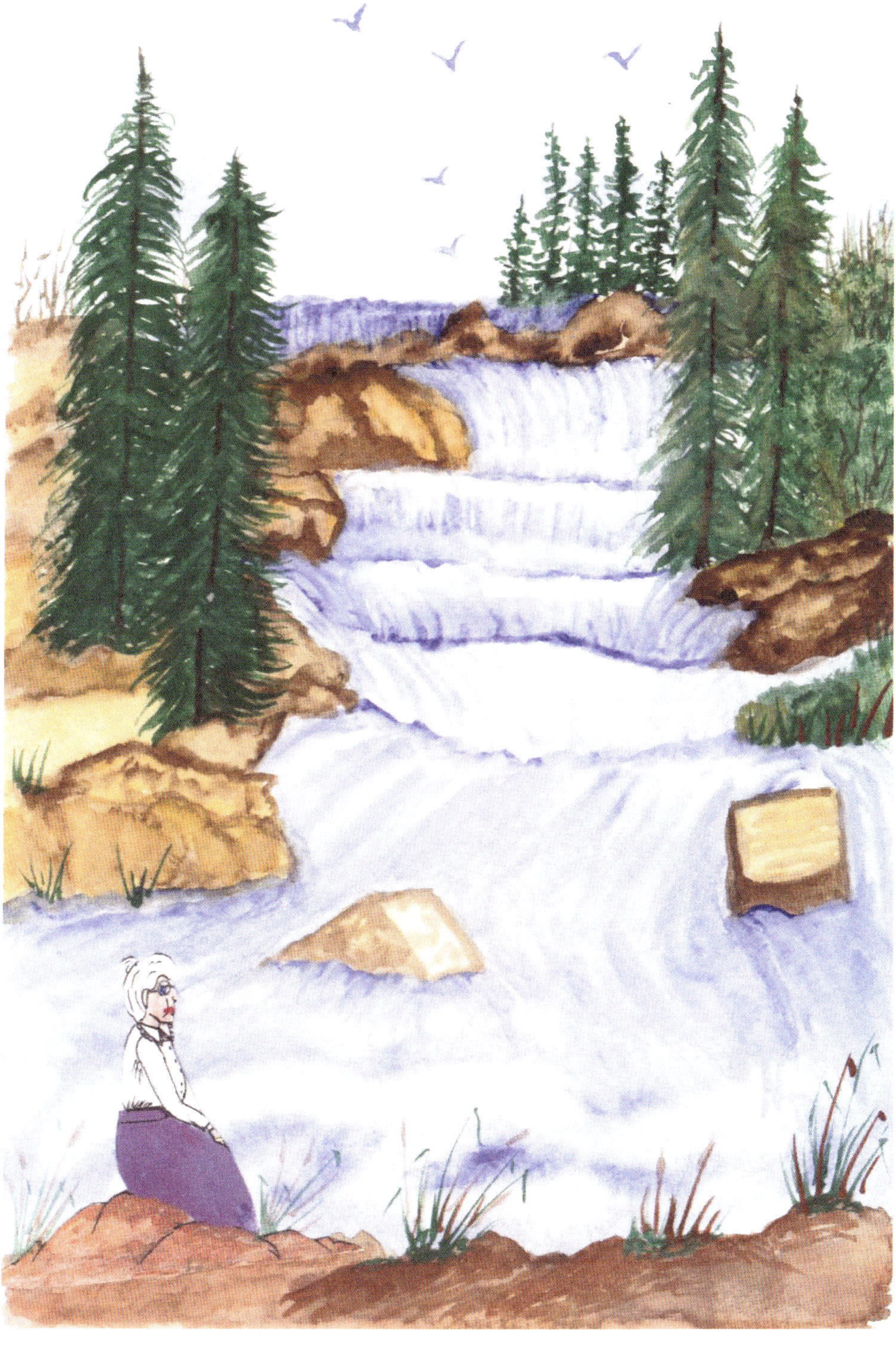

They climbed to the top and sat on an old log to enjoy the view. "We can see for miles and miles", said Nana. "Look down at the waterfall. It's a rainbow!"

Peter said, "I have to go back to the farm now. I will see you again soon."

"Wait!" shouted Nana. "There is something missing."

"What is it?" Peter asked.

"Where is my family? Where are the ones that came before me? Where is my mother, my father, my grandparents, aunts, uncles and friends?"

Peter pointed and said, "Look down by the waterfalls."

Nana turned around and saw a large group of people waving and calling her name. Nana was overjoyed to see everyone. They all waved for her to come down.

Nana was so happy and knew this truly was a wonderful heaven.

"Now all is truly blessed and happy"

THE BEGINNING…

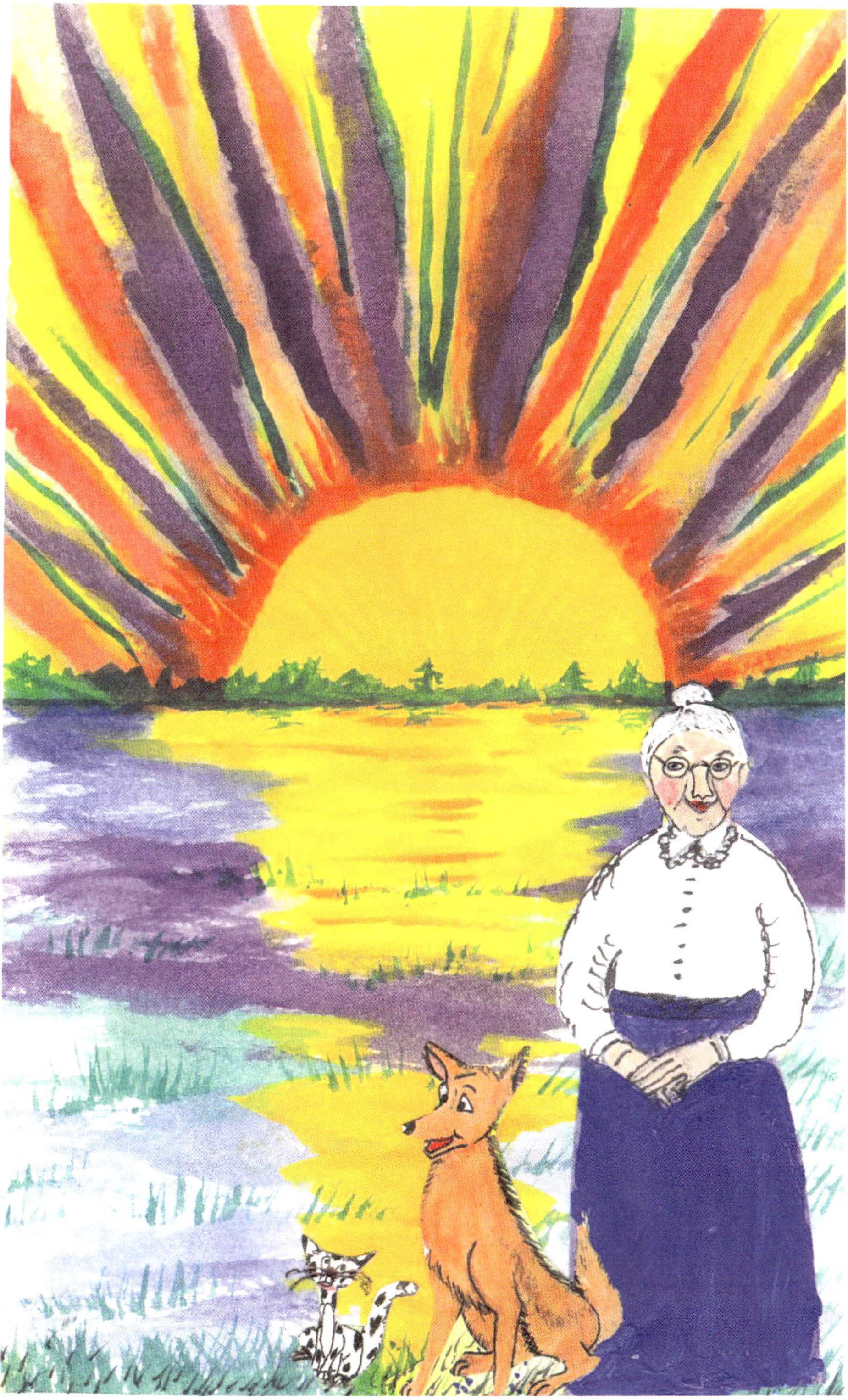

Printed in Great Britain
by Amazon